ROYAL COURT

Royal Court Theatre presents

MY CHILD

by **Mike Bartlett**

First performance at the Royal Court Jerwood Theatre Downstairs,
Sloane Square, London on 3 May 2007.

supported by

JERWOOD
NEW PLAYWRIGHTS

14 June – 21 July

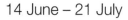

the pain and the itch

by Bruce Norris

AN INFECTIOUS COMEDY

A cosy family Thanksgiving dinner for six. Someone – or something – is leaving bite marks in the avocados. Clay and Kelly's daughter Kayla has an itch and Carol can't remember who played Gandhi.

In his first UK production, American writer Bruce Norris takes a withering look at phoney liberal values in this hilarious social satire.

Direction
Dominic Cooke

Design
Robert Innes Hopkins

Lighting
Hugh Vanstone

Sound
Paul Arditti

Cast includes
Matthew Macfadyen

500 tickets £5 for 25s and under*

020 7565 5000
www.royalcourttheatre.com
Royal Court Theatre, Sloane Square, London SW1

ARTS COUNCIL ENGLAND

MY CHILD

by **Mike Bartlett**

Father **Richard Albrecht**
Child **Adam Arnold**
Mother **Jan Chappell**
Karl **Adam James**
Older Woman **Sara Kestelman**
Another Man **James Livingstone**
Man **Ben Miles**
Another Woman **Antoinette Tagoe**
Young Woman **Jodie Taibi**
Other Woman **Romy Tennant**
Woman **Lia Williams**

Director **Sacha Wares**
Designer **Miriam Buether**
Lighting Designer **Johanna Town**
Sound Designer **Ian Dickinson**
Choreographer **Juha Marsalo**
Assistant Director **Amy Hodge**
Casting **Amy Ball**
Production Managers **Sue Bird, Paul Handley**
Stage Manager **Richard Llewelyn**
Deputy Stage Manager **Tamara Albachari**
Assistant Stage Manager **Sarah Lyndon**
Costume Supervisor **Jackie Orton**
Rayne Fellowship Observer **Luca Silvestrini**
Dialect Coach **Jan Hayden Rowles**
Company Voice Work **Patsy Rodenburg**
Set Built By **Miraculous Engineering**
Set Painted By **Charlotte Gainey**

With thanks to Jenny Hall for her support of this production.

The Royal Court and Stage Management would also like to thank the following: Duncan Campbell at Max Fordham, CBS Outdoors, Clarks Shoes, Wheelchair courtesy of Keep Able, Lifes2Good, Radio Control Car courtesy of Nikko Toys, Nourkrin Man, Vitabiotics, Volvo, Worcester Bosch Group.

THE COMPANY

Mike Bartlett (writer)
Mike was part of the YWP group in 2005. This is his first play for the stage. His play, Not Talking, was broadcast on BBC Radio in 2006.

Richard Albrecht
For the Royal Court: Ashes and Sand.
Theatre includes: Beauty and the Beast (Jackson's Lane); Perfect Pitch (Derby Playhouse); Road to Hell (Birmingham Rep Studio); Happy as a Sandbag (Ambassador's); Joseph and his Technicolour Dreamcoat, A Streetcar Named Desire (Leicester Haymarket); The Rise and Fall of Little Voice (Derby Playhouse); Twelfth Night (Colchester Mercury); Woolf (Traverse, Edinburgh/tour); The Tempest (Salisbury Playhouse); Sweet Sessions (Shared Experience).
Television includes: Where the Heart Is, Coronation Street, Doctors, The Last Detective, Blue Dove, Mersey Beat, The Glass, East Enders, Casualty, Dalziel and Pascoe, London Bridge, Births Marriages and Deaths, Out of Hours, Mr White Goes to Westminster, Heartbeat VII, Soldier Soldier VII, Brookside, Goodnight Sweetheart, Emmerdale, Holding On, The Vet.
Film includes: The Man Who Cried, Jude the Obscure.

Adam Arnold
Theatre includes: Hecuba (Donmar); Putting It Together (St James' Theatre).
Film includes: Hibernation.

Miriam Buether (designer)
For the Royal Court: The Wonderful World of Dissocia (National Theatre of Scotland tour), Way to Heaven
Other theatre includes: generations (Young Vic); Pool (No Water) (Frantic Assembly); Realism (National Theatre of Scotland/EIF); Long Time Dead (Paines Plough/Drum); The Bee (Soho); Unprotected (Liverpool Everyman); trade (RSC); After the End (Paines Plough/Bush); The Death of Klinghoffer (Scottish Opera); Platform (ICA); Guantanamo (Tricycle); People Next Door (Traverse); The Dumb Waiter (Oxford Playhouse); Red Demon (Young Vic); Bintou (Arcola); Eskimo Sisters (Southwark Playhouse).
Dance includes: Outsight, Tender Hooks (Gulbenkian Foundation, Lisbon); Toot and Possibly Six (Les Grand Ballets Canadiens de Montreal); Track (Scottish Dance Theatre); Body of Poetry (Komische Oper, Berlin); 7DS (Sadler's Wells).
Awards include: 1999 Linbury Prize for Stage Design.

Jan Chappell
For the Royal Court: Three More Sleepless Nights,

Light Shining in Buckinghamshire (& Joint Stock), Fair Slaughter, No End of Blame (& Oxford); Ubu Roi, Voysey Inheritance.
Other theatre includes: Guantanamo (Congress/ Tricycle/Ambassador's); Jackets (Young Vic); Les Liaisons Dangereuses (PW Prods No1 Tour); The Colour of Justice, Half the Picture (Tricycle); Romeo and Juliet, Macbeth, The General from America, As You Like It, Richard II, Love's Labours Lost, Comrades, The Beast (RSC); Everest Hotel (Bush); On the Rocks (Mermaid); Macbeth (Nottingham); The Duchess of Malfi (Oxford Playhouse); Grave Dancer (Finborough); Playboy of the Western World, St Joan (Salisbury); Caravaggio (Traverse, Edinburgh); Romeo and Juliet (Haymarket); Othello, Heartbreak House (Stoke on Trent).
Television includes: Rosemary & Thyme, Doctors, Spooks, New Tricks, Holby City, The Colour of Justice, The Alchemist, Planet Mirth, Half the Picture, Madson, Faith, House of Elliot, Pie in the Sky, Lovejoy, Casualty, Anna Lee, Inspector Alleyn, Running Late, The Bill, Tales from Hollywood, Boon, After the War, The Soldier & Death, Mr Palfrey of Westminster, Reilly, Crown Court, Blakes Seven.
Film includes: Basic Instinct 2, Low Tide, Green Fingers, Virgin and the Gipsy, The Devils, Jesus of Nazareth.

Ian Dickinson (sound designer)
For the Royal Court: The Eleventh Capital, The Seagull, Krapp's Last Tape, Piano/Forte, Rock 'n' Roll (& Duke of York's), Motortown, Rainbow Kiss, The Winterling, Alice Trilogy, Fewer Emergencies, Way to Heaven, The Woman Before, Stoning Mary (& Drum Theatre, Plymouth), Breathing Corpses, Wild East, Dumb Show, Shining City (& Gate, Dublin), Lucky Dog, Blest Be the Tie (with Talawa), Ladybird, Notes on Falling Leaves, Loyal Women, The Sugar Syndrome, Blood, Playing the Victim (with Told By an Idiot), Fallout, Flesh Wound, Hitchcock Blonde (& Lyric), Black Milk, Crazyblackmuthafuckin'self, Caryl Churchill Shorts, Push Up, Fucking Games, Herons.
Other theatre includes: King Of Hearts (Out of Joint); Love and Money (Young Vic); Much Ado About Nothing (redesign, RSC/Novello); Pillars of the Community (National); A Few Good Men (Haymarket); Dr Faustus (Chichester Festival Theatre); The Magic Carpet (Lyric Hammersmith); Port, As You Like It, Poor Superman, Martin Yesterday, Fast Food, Coyote Ugly (Royal Exchange, Manchester); Night of the Soul (RSC/Barbican); Eyes of the Kappa (Gate); Crime & Punishment in Dalston (Arcola); Search & Destroy (New End); The Whore's Dream (RSC/Edinburgh).
Ian is Head of Sound at the Royal Court.

Amy Hodge (assistant director)
Theatre includes, as director: The Ethics of Progress (Unlimited Theatre/Oxford Playhouse); The Tempest (Orange Tree Theatre schools tour); Kick for Touch (Orange Tree Theatre); Theatre of Change (Congrieve Room, West Yorkshire Playhouse); Influenced (Etcetera); Vagina Monologues (Leeds City Variety Music Hall). Theatre includes, as assistant director: Tangle (Unlimited Theatre co.); The Hoxton Story (The Red Room).
Amy was trainee director at the Orange Tree Theatre 2005-2006.

Adam James
Theatre includes: French Without Tears (English Touring Theatre); Rabbit (Trafalgar Studio/Old Red Lion); Lone Star Mark One (Salisbury Playhouse); The Importance of Being Earnest (No 1 tour); Original Sin (Sheffield Crucible); Time and the Conways, Snake in Fridge, King Lear, Poor Superman (Royal Exchange); Glass Menagerie (Minerva); Chimes at Midnight (Chichester); Unseen Hand, Lone Star, Private Wars (Bristol Old Vic); A View from the Bridge (Theatre Royal, York); Tamburlaine the Great (RSC); Coriolanus (NYT). Television includes: The Commander, Judge John Deed, Desperados, The Amazing Mrs Pritchard, Waking the Dead, Rise and Fall, Shiny Shiny Bright New Hole in My Heart, Love Soup, Casualty, Meucci, England, Reversals, As If, Trust, After Hours, The Lost Battalion, Murder on the Orient Express, Band of Brothers, I Saw You, Life of the Party, Tenth Kingdom, Let Them Eat Cake, Silent Witness, Island II, The Bill, Sharpe's Regiment, Cold Lazarus. Film includes: Mother of Tears, Road to Guantanamo, De-Lovely, Prima Dammi Un Baccio, A Family Man, Three Blind Mice, It's Not You It's Me, High Heels and Low Life, Gregory's 2 Girls, Forbidden Territory.

Sara Kestelman
Theatre includes: The Shape of Metal (Abbey, Dublin); Hamlet (National); Copenhagen (National/West End); Three Tall Women, Lettice & Lovage (Wyndham's); Cabaret, Nine (Donmar); Fiddler on the Roof (Palladium); Some Sunny Day (Hampstead); Sarrasine (Lyric Hammersmith); The Cherry Orchard (Gate, Dublin); Three Sisters (Greenwich/West End); All About Me! (own songs and poems – New York/Dublin/National/King's Head); A Two Hander (published poems of Sara Kestelman and Susan Penhaligan – Hampstead); extensive work with the National and RSC. Television includes: Instinct, Rome, Casualty, Midsomer Murders, Ultimate Force, Trial & Retribution, Relic Hunter, Mind Games, Anna Karenina, Tom Jones, Invasion Earth, Kavanagh QC, Ruth Rendell Mysteries.
Film includes: Lady Jane, Zardoz, Lisztomania, Break of Day, Ex Memoria.
Radio includes: Hitler in Therapy, An Ideal Husband, Bleak House, Fiddler on the Roof, Book at Bedtime (for which Sara adapted Full House), Modem Gal (written & performed).
Awards include: 1994 Olivier & The Clarence Derwent Best Supporting Performance in a Musical for Cabaret; 2005 Best Actress Radio Award for Hitler in Therapy.

James Livingstone
Theatre includes: Platform (ICA); Of Walking in Ice (site-specific); Inner City (Artangel); Too Far to Walk (King's Head); Playing from the Heart (Lyceum, Edinburgh); Sweet Love Remembered (Globe); Carmen (Newcastle Playhouse); The Thirst (Leicester Haymarket); Beauty and the Beast (New Vic, Stoke); Picture of Dorian Gray (Theatre Royal, Bury St Edmunds); The Libertine (Pentameters); The Man With Three Hats (Turnhalle, Kings Cross); Half a Life (Civic Hall, Leeds); May Day (site-specific).
Television includes: Darien Disaster, Popcorn, Trial and Retribution, Trail of Guilt, Make my Day, Bad Company, The Bill, Kavanagh QC, London's Burning.
Film includes: Savage Hearts.
James is the voice of Headhunter for Playstation2.

Juha Marsalo (choreographer)
Dance performance includes: Dall'interno (Carolyn Carlson Co.); Inasmuch as the Life is Borrowed, Inspite of Wishing and Wanting, What The Body Doesn't Remember, Les Porteuses des Mauvaises Nouvelles (Wim Vandekeybus's Ultima Vez Co.).
Choreography includes: Etude pour 4 Mouvements, Ethogramme, 4 Propositions pour un Solo (L'Expérience Harmaat); Isä, Oiva, Shocking, Prologue d'une scène d'amour, Scène d'Amour, Perle (Juha Marsalo Co.).

Ben Miles
Theatre includes: Richard II (Old Vic); Hand in Hand to the Promised Land (Hampstead); The Cherry Orchard, The London Cuckolds, Mary Stuart, Macbeth, Trelawny of the Wells, Fuente Ovejuna (National); The Tower (Almeida); The Miser (Chichester); Two Gentleman of Verona, Hamlet, Romeo and Juliet, Have, Ispanka (RSC); The Winter's Tale (Young Vic); The Tempest (Phoebus Cart); A Woman of No Importance (Cambridge Theatre Co.); Scars (Lyric Hammersmith); Chiefly Yourselves (NYT).
Television includes: To Be First, Bon Voyage, After Thomas, Under the Greenwood Tree, The Government Inspector, Mr Harvey Lights a Candle, Spin, A Thing Called Love, Prime Suspect,

Love Again, The Forsythe Saga, Cold Feet, The Innocent, Coupling, Rough Treatment, Reach for the Moon, The Life and Crimes of William Palmer, The Round Tower, Measure for Measure.
Film includes: V for Vendetta, Three Blind Mice, Affair of the Necklace, Keep the Asperdistra Flying, Wings of the Dove, Imagine Me and You, Paris, Brixton.

Antoinette Tagoe
Theatre includes: Lion and the Jewel (UK national tour); Under One Roof (V&A/Soho).
Radio includes: Nine Circles.

Jodie Taibi
Jodie is currently in her final year of training at Webber Douglas and Central School, graduating in July 2007.
This is her first professional production.

Romy Tennant
Theatre includes: Love Song (New Ambassador's); Festen (Almeida/tour); The Miserable Failure of Bernard Comiskey (Dublin Fringe Festival); The Treason Show (Komedia, Brighton); Dinner (Wyndham's); Frog Prince (Wimbledon Studio/ Edinburgh Fringe); Miss Caroline (White Bear); A Midsummer Night's Dream (Open Air Tour); Shakers (Mansfield Palace); Scratch (20:21 Productions, UK Tour); Dimaa (BAC).
Radio includes: New Adventures of Doctor Who, Earthsearch, And When You Sleep You Remind Me of the Dead.
Film includes: Danny Boy (short), Cool Water, Heading South, Wish List (short).

Johanna Town (lighting designer)
For the Royal Court: Over 50 productions, including – Scenes from the Back of Beyond, My Name is Rachel Corrie (& West End/Galway Festival/Edinburgh Festival/Minetta Lane, New York), Rainbow Kiss, The Winterling, The Woman Before, Way To Heaven, A Girl in a Car With a Man, Under the Whaleback, The Kitchen, O Go My Man (with Out of Joint), Talking to Terrorists (with Out of Joint), Shopping and Fucking (with Out of Joint/ West End), The Steward of Christendom (with Out of Joint/Broadway).
Other theatre includes: Guantanamo (Tricycle/ West End/New York); Rose (National/New York); Arabian Nights, Our Lady of Sligo (New York); Little Malcolm and His Struggle Against the Eunuchs (West End/Hampstead); Feelgood, Top Girls, Via Dolorosa, Beautiful Thing (West End); To Kill A Mocking Bird (Birmingham Rep/tour); The Glassroom (Hampstead); The Overwhelming, The Permanent Way, She Stoops to Conquer (Out

of Joint/National); Macbeth (Out of Joint world tour); In Praise of Love (Chichester); Dead Funny (West Yorkshire Playhouse); All the Ordinary Angels (Royal Exchange); East Coast Chicken Supper (Traverse); Helen of Troy (ATC); How Love is Spelt (Bush); I.D. (Almeida/BBC3); Badnuff (Soho); The Dumb Waiter (Oxford); Popcorn (Liverpool Playhouse).
Johanna is Head of Lighting at the Royal Court.

Sacha Wares (director)
For the Royal Court: Credible Witness.
Other theatre includes: generations (Young Vic); trade (RSC/Soho); Platform (ICA); A Number (Theatre Project Tokyo); Guantanamo (co-directed with Nicolas Kent, Tricycle/West End/New York); Bintou (Arcola); Six Degrees of Separation (Sheffield Crucible); Pera Palas (NT Springboards at The Gate); One Life and Counting (Bush).
Awards include: Jerwood Director's Award 2005.
Sacha is an Associate Director at the Royal Court.

Lia Williams
For the Royal Court: King Lear, Oleanna (& Duke of York's).
Other theatre includes: Postcards from America, As You Like It (RSC); Eccentricities of a Nightingale (Gate, Dublin); Mappa Mundi (National); The Homecoming (Gate, Dublin/West End/New York); Celebration/The Room (Almeida/New York); The Lover & The Collection (Donmar); Skylight (National/West End/Broadway); The Revenger's Comedies (The Strand); Body Language (Stephen Joseph); Daisy Pulls it Off (Globe).
Television includes: May 33rd, The Lives of Animals, The Russian Bride, Bad Blood, Imogen's Face, A Shot through the Heart, The Uninvited, Flowers of the Forest, Seaforth, Mr Wroe's Virgins.
Film includes: Jonathan Toomey, Girl from Rio, The King is Alive, Different for Girls, The Fifth Province, Firelight, Dirty Weekend.
As director, film includes: Feathers (short), The Stronger (short).
Radio includes: Dr Glas, Snow, Scenes of Seduction, Raj Quartet, Japanese Gothic Tales, Easy Virtue, Breath of God, Season's Greeting, Red Room, The Idiot, Drop Dead Gorgeous, Lady Chatterley's Lover.
Awards include: New York Theatre World Outstanding Broadway Debut Award for Skylight; FIPA Best Actress Award 2002 for The Russian Bride; Critics' Circle Most Promising Newcomer Award and SWET Best Comedy Performance Award 1992 for The Revenger's Comedies; Irish Theatre Awards Best Actress for Eccentricities of a Nightingale.

THE ENGLISH STAGE COMPANY
AT THE ROYAL COURT

The English Stage Company at the Royal Court opened in 1956 as a subsidised theatre producing new British plays, international plays and some classical revivals.

The first artistic director George Devine aimed to create a writers' theatre, 'a place where the dramatist is acknowledged as the fundamental creative force in the theatre and where the play is more important than the actors, the director, the designer'. The urgent need was to find a contemporary style in which the play, the acting, direction and design are all combined. He believed that 'the battle will be a long one to continue to create the right conditions for writers to work in'.

Devine aimed to discover 'hard-hitting, uncompromising writers whose plays are stimulating, provocative and exciting'. The Royal Court production of John Osborne's Look Back in Anger in May 1956 is now seen as the decisive starting point of modern British drama and the policy created a new generation of British playwrights. The first wave included John Osborne, Arnold Wesker, John Arden, Ann Jellicoe, N F Simpson and Edward Bond. Early seasons included new international plays by Bertolt Brecht, Eugène Ionesco, Samuel Beckett and Jean-Paul Sartre.

The theatre started with the 400-seat proscenium arch Theatre Downstairs, and in 1969 opened a second theatre, the 60-seat studio Theatre Upstairs. Some productions transfer to the West End, such as Tom Stoppard's Rock 'n' Roll, My Name is Rachel Corrie, Terry Johnson's Hitchcock Blonde, Caryl Churchill's Far Away and Conor McPherson's The Weir. Recent touring productions include Sarah Kane's 4.48 Psychosis (US tour) and Ché Walker's Flesh Wound (Galway Arts Festival). The Royal Court also co-produces plays which transfer to the West End or tour internationally, such as Conor McPherson's Shining City (with Gate Theatre, Dublin), Sebastian Barry's The Steward of Christendom and Mark Ravenhill's Shopping and Fucking (with Out of Joint), Martin McDonagh's The Beauty Queen Of Leenane (with Druid), Ayub Khan Din's East is East (with Tamasha).

Since 1994 the Royal Court's artistic policy has again been vigorously directed to finding and producing a new generation of playwrights. The writers include Joe Penhall, Rebecca Prichard, Michael Wynne, Nick Grosso, Judy Upton, Meredith Oakes, Sarah Kane, Anthony Neilson, Judith Johnson, James Stock, Jez Butterworth, Marina Carr, Phyllis Nagy, Simon Block, Martin McDonagh, Mark Ravenhill, Ayub Khan Din, Tamantha Hammerschlag,

photo: Stephen Cummiiskey

Jess Walters, Ché Walker, Conor McPherson, Simon Stephens, Richard Bean, Roy Williams, Gary Mitchell, Mick Mahoney, Rebecca Gilman, Christopher Shinn, Kia Corthron, David Gieselmann, Marius von Mayenburg, David Eldridge, Leo Butler, Zinnie Harris, Grae Cleugh, Roland Schimmelpfennig, Chloe Moss, DeObia Oparei, Enda Walsh, Vassily Sigarev, the Presnyakov Brothers, Marcos Barbosa, Lucy Prebble, John Donnelly, Clare Pollard, Robin French, Elyzabeth Gregory Wilder, Rob Evans, Laura Wade, Debbie Tucker Green, Levi David Addai and Simon Farquhar. This expanded programme of new plays has been made possible through the support of A.S.K. Theater Projects and the Skirball Foundation, The Jerwood Charity, the American Friends of the Royal Court Theatre and (in 1994/5 and 1999) the National Theatre Studio.

The refurbished theatre in Sloane Square opened in February 2000, with a policy still inspired by the first artistic director George Devine. The Royal Court is an international theatre for new plays and new playwrights, and the work shapes contemporary drama in Britain and overseas.

The Royal Court's long and successful history of innovation has been built by generations of gifted and imaginative individuals. For information on the many exciting ways you can help support the theatre, please contact the Development Department on 020 7565 5079.

AWARDS FOR
THE ROYAL COURT

Martin McDonagh won the 1996 George Devine Award, the 1996 Writers' Guild Best Fringe Play Award, the 1996 Critics' Circle Award and the 1996 Evening Standard Award for Most Promising Playwright for The Beauty Queen of Leenane. Marina Carr won the 19th Susan Smith Blackburn Prize (1996/7) for Portia Coughlan. Conor McPherson won the 1997 George Devine Award, the 1997 Critics' Circle Award and the 1997 Evening Standard Award for Most Promising Playwright for The Weir. Ayub Khan Din won the 1997 Writers' Guild Awards for Best West End Play and New Writer of the Year and the 1996 John Whiting Award for East is East (co-production with Tamasha).

Martin McDonagh's The Beauty Queen of Leenane (co-production with Druid Theatre Company) won four 1998 Tony Awards including Garry Hynes for Best Director. Eugene Ionesco's The Chairs (co-production with Theatre de Complicite) was nominated for six Tony awards. David Hare won the 1998 Time Out Live Award for Outstanding Achievement and six awards in New York including the Drama League, Drama Desk and New York Critics Circle Award for Via Dolorosa. Sarah Kane won the 1998 Arts Foundation Fellowship in Playwriting. Rebecca Prichard won the 1998 Critics' Circle Award for Most Promising Playwright for Yard Gal (co-production with Clean Break).

Conor McPherson won the 1999 Olivier Award for Best New Play for The Weir. The Royal Court won the 1999 ITI Award for Excellence in International Theatre. Sarah Kane's Cleansed was judged Best Foreign Language Play in 1999 by Theater Heute in Germany. Gary Mitchell won the 1999 Pearson Best Play Award for Trust. Rebecca Gilman was joint winner of the 1999 George Devine Award and won the 1999 Evening Standard Award for Most Promising Playwright for The Glory of Living.

In 1999, the Royal Court won the European theatre prize New Theatrical Realities, presented at Taormina Arte in Sicily, for its efforts in recent years in discovering and producing the work of young British dramatists.

Roy Williams and Gary Mitchell were joint winners of the George Devine Award 2000 for Most Promising Playwright for Lift Off and The Force of Change respectively. At the Barclays Theatre Awards 2000 presented by the TMA, Richard Wilson won the Best Director Award for David Gieselmann's Mr Kolpert and Jeremy Herbert won the Best Designer Award for Sarah Kane's 4.48 Psychosis. Gary Mitchell won the Evening Standard's Charles Wintour Award 2000 for Most Promising Playwright for The Force of Change. Stephen Jeffreys' I Just Stopped by to See the Man won an AT&T: On Stage Award 2000.

David Eldridge's Under the Blue Sky won the Time Out Live Award 2001 for Best New Play in the West End. Leo Butler won the George Devine Award 2001 for Most Promising Playwright for Redundant. Roy Williams won the Evening Standard's Charles Wintour Award 2001 for Most Promising Playwright for Clubland. Grae Cleugh won the 2001 Olivier Award for Most Promising Playwright for Fucking Games.

Richard Bean was joint winner of the George Devine Award 2002 for Most Promising Playwright for Under the Whaleback. Caryl Churchill won the 2002 Evening Standard Award for Best New Play for A Number. Vassily Sigarev won the 2002 Evening Standard Charles Wintour Award for Most Promising Playwright for Plasticine. Ian MacNeil won the 2002 Evening Standard Award for Best Design for A Number and Plasticine. Peter Gill won the 2002 Critics' Circle Award for Best New Play for The York Realist (English Touring Theatre). Ché Walker won the 2003 George Devine Award for Most Promising Playwright for Flesh Wound. Lucy Prebble won the 2003 Critics' Circle Award and the 2004 George Devine Award for Most Promising Playwright, and the TMA Theatre Award 2004 for Best New Play for The Sugar Syndrome. Richard Bean won the 2005 Critics' Circle Award for Best New Play for Harvest. Laura Wade won the 2005 Critics' Circle Award for Most Promising Playwright and the 2005 Pearson Best Play Award for Breathing Corpses. The 2006 Whatsonstage Theatregoers' Choice Award for Best New Play was won by My Name is Rachel Corrie. The 2005 Evening Standard Special Award was given to the Royal Court 'for making and changing theatrical history this last half century'.

Tom Stoppard's Rock 'n' Roll won the 2006 Evening Standard Award for Best Play and the 2006 Critics' Circle Award for Best Play.

ROYAL COURT BOOKSHOP

The Royal Court bookshop offers a range of contemporary plays and publications on the theory and practice of modern drama. The staff specialise in assisting with the selection of audition monologues and scenes. Royal Court playtexts from past and present productions cost £2.

The Bookshop is situated to the right of the stairs leading to the ROYAL COURT CAFE BAR.

Monday to Friday 3 – 10pm
Saturday 2.30 – 10pm
(Closed shortly every evening from 7.45 to 8.15pm)

For information tel: 020 7565 5024
or email: bookshop@royalcourttheatre.com

Books can also be ordered from our website
www.royalcourttheatre.com

PROGRAMME SUPPORTERS

The Royal Court (English Stage Company Ltd) receives its principal funding from Arts Council England, London. It is also supported financially by a wide range of private companies, charitable and public bodies, and earns the remainder of its income from the box office and its own trading activities.

The Genesis Foundation supports the Royal Court's work with International Playwrights.

The Jerwood Charity supports new plays by new playwrights through the Jerwood New Playwrights series.

The Artistic Director's Chair is supported by a lead grant from The Peter Jay Sharp Foundation, contributing to the activities of the Artistic Director's office. Over the past nine years the BBC has supported the Gerald Chapman Fund for directors.

American Friends of the Royal Court are primarily focused on raising funds to enable the theatre to produce new work by emerging American writers. AFRCT has also supported the participation of young artists in the Royal Court's acclaimed International Residency. Contact: 001-212-946-5724.

ROYAL COURT
DEVELOPMENT BOARD
John Ayton
Anthony Burton
Sindy Caplan (Vice-Chair)
Gavin Casey FCA
Cas Donald
Allie Esiri
AC Farstad
Celeste Fenichel
Tamara Ingram
Emma Marsh
Gavin Neath
Mark Robinson
William Russell (Chair)

PUBLIC FUNDING
Arts Council England, London
British Council
London Challenge
Royal Borough of Kensington & Chelsea

TRUSTS AND FOUNDATIONS
American Friends of the Royal Court Theatre
Bulldog Prinsep Theatrical Fund
Gerald Chapman Fund
Columbia Foundation
The Sidney & Elizabeth Corob Charitable Trust
Cowley Charitable Trust
The Dorset Foundation
The Ronald Duncan Literary Foundation
The Edwin Fox Foundation
The Foyle Foundation
Francis Finlay
The Garfield Weston Foundation
Genesis Foundation
Sheila Hancock
Jerwood Charity
Lloyds TSB Foundation for England and Wales
Lynn Foundation
John Lyon's Charity
The Magowan Family Foundation
The Laura Pels Foundation

The Martin Bowley Charitable Trust
The Peggy Ramsay Foundation
Quercus Charitable Trust
Rose Foundation
Royal College of Psychiatrists
The Royal Victoria Hall Foundation
The Peter Jay Sharp Foundation
Wates Foundation
Michael J Zamkow & Sue E Berman Charitable Trust

SPONSORS AND BUSINESS MEMBERS
Aviva Plc
BBC
Coutts & Co
Grey London
John Malkovich/Uncle Kimono
Kudos Film and Television
Lazard
Merrill Lynch
Pemberton Greenish
Simons Muirhead & Burton
Vanity Fair

PRODUCTION SYNDICATE
Anonymous
Dianne & Michael Bienes
Ms Kay Ellen Consolver
Mrs Philip Donald
Daniel & Joanna Friel
John Garfield
Peter & Edna Goldstein
Daisy Prince
William & Hilary Russell
Jon & NoraLee Sedmak
Ian & Carol Sellars

INDIVIDUAL MEMBERS
Patrons
Anonymous
Katie Bradford
Simon & Karen Day
Cas Donald
Tom & Simone Fenton
Tim Fosberry
John Garfield

Nick Gould
Sue & Don Guiney
Charles & Elizabeth Handy
Jan Harris
Jack & Linda Keenan
Pawel & Sarah Kisielewski
Kathryn Ludlow
Deborah & Stephen Marquardt
Duncan Matthews QC
Jill & Paul Ruddock
Ian & Carol Sellars
Jan & Michael Topham
Richard Wilson OBE

Benefactors
Anonymous
Martha Allfrey
Amanda Attard-Manché
Varian Ayers & Gary Knisely
John & Anoushka Ayton
Mr & Mrs Gavin Casey
Sindy & Jonathan Caplan
Jeremy Conway & Nicola Van Gelder
Robyn Durie
Hugo Eddis
Joachim Fleury
Beverley Gee
Lydia & Manfred Gorvy
Claire Guinness
Sam & Caroline Haubold
Nicholas Josefowitz
David Kaskell & Christopher Teano
Peter & Maria Kellner
Colette & Peter Levy
Larry & Peggy Levy
Barbara Minto
Elaine Potter
Kadee Robbins
Mark Robinson
William & Hilary Russell
Lois Sieff OBE
Brian D Smith
Sue Stapely
Carl & Martha Tack
Amanda Vail
Sir Robert & Lady Wilson
Nick Wheeler

Associates
Act IV
Anonymous
Alan Brodie
Clive & Helena Butler
Gaynor Buxton
Cynthia Corbett
Margaret Cowper
Andrew Cryer
Celeste Fenichel
Charlotte & Nick Fraser
Gillian Frumkin
Julia Fuller
Sara Galbraith & Robert Ham
Vivien Goodwin
Linda Grosse
Lady Lever
Mr Watcyn Lewis
David Marks
Nicola McFarland
Gavin & Ann Neath
Janet & Michael Orr
S. Osman
Pauline Pinder
William Poeton CBE & Barbara Poeton
Gail Steele
Nick Steidl
Silke Ziehl

JERWOOD
NEW PLAYWRIGHTS

Since 1994 Jerwood New Playwrights has contributed to 53 new plays at the Royal Court including Joe Penhall's SOME VOICES, Mark Ravenhill's SHOPPING AND FUCKING (co-production with Out of Joint), Ayub Khan Din's EAST IS EAST (co-production with Tamasha), Martin McDonagh's THE BEAUTY QUEEN OF LEENANE (co-production with Druid Theatre Company), Conor McPherson's THE WEIR, Nick Grosso's REAL CLASSY AFFAIR, Sarah Kane's 4.48 PSYCHOSIS, Gary Mitchell's THE FORCE OF CHANGE, David Eldridge's UNDER THE BLUE SKY, David Harrower's PRESENCE, Simon Stephens' HERONS, Roy Williams' CLUBLAND, Leo Butler's REDUNDANT, Michael Wynne's THE PEOPLE ARE FRIENDLY, David Greig's OUTLYING ISLANDS, Zinnie Harris' NIGHTINGALE AND CHASE, Grae Cleugh's FUCKING GAMES, Rona Munro's IRON, Richard Bean's UNDER THE WHALEBACK, Ché Walker's FLESH WOUND, Roy Williams' FALLOUT, Mick Mahoney's FOOD CHAIN, Ayub Khan Din's NOTES ON FALLING LEAVES, Leo Butler's LUCKY DOG, Simon Stephens' COUNTRY MUSIC, Laura Wade's BREATHING CORPSES, Debbie Tucker Green's STONING MARY, David Eldridge's INCOMPLETE AND RANDOM ACTS OF KINDNESS, Gregory Burke's ON TOUR, Stella Feehily's O GO MY MAN, Simon Stephens' MOTORTOWN, Simon Farquhar's RAINBOW KISS and April de Angelis, Stella Feehily, Tanika Gupta, Chloe Moss and Laura Wade's CATCH.

In 2007 Jerwood New Playwrights has also supported THAT FACE by Polly Stenham.

The Jerwood Charitable Foundation is a registered charity dedicated to imaginative and responsible funding of the arts and other areas of human endeavour and excellence.

Simon Farquhar's RAINBOW KISS
(photo: John Haynes)

Simon Stephens' MOTORTOWN
(photo: Robert Workman)

FOR THE ROYAL COURT

ALMEIDA
THEATRE

11 May – 30 June 2007
European premiere

Big White Fog

By Theodore Ward

**One man's fight to
keep his dreams alive
and his family together**

Director Michael Attenborough
Design Jonathan Fensom
Lighting Tim Mitchell
Sound John Leonard

Box Office 020 7359 4404
www.almeida.co.uk

My Child

To my family

Thanks to Dominic Cooke, Jessica Cooper,
Amy Sackville, Dan Snelgrove, Simon Stephens,
Jeremy Taylor, John Terry, Lyndsey Turner,
Graham Whybrow, Simon, Duncan, Rachael,
Morgan, Nick, the YWP, and to Sacha Wares,
Miriam Buether, and all at the Royal Court Theatre,
who have been so supportive of this play
and encouraging of me as a writer

Characters

Man
Mother
Older Woman
Woman
Child
Other Woman
Young Woman
Another Woman
Another Man
Father
Karl

The audience and actors come into the space together. It is not clear who the actors are at first.

Actors can go anywhere in the space.

No actors should enter or leave the theatre during the performance.

Note

/ means the next speech begins at that point.

– means the next line interrupts.

. . . at the end of a speech means it trails off. On its own, it indicates a pressure, expectation or desire to speak.

A speech with no written dialogue indicates a character deliberately remaining silent.

Blank space between speeches in the dialogue indicates time drifting on with slightly less happening for a moment.

Darkness.

Man   Mum?

Mother   Shh.

Older Woman   Love?

Woman   Shh.

Man   What do I do?

Mother   Darling.

Child   Mum.

Man   Shhh.

Child   Mummy.

Man   Shush.

Excuse me.

Sorry.

Lights up.

Child   My arm hurts.

Man   Shut up.

Child   My arm hurts bad.

Man   Look, I'm really trying here. I'm trying to do my best.

Woman   He looks ill to me.

Man   We had a nice time.

Woman   Did you?

Man   Yes.

Woman   He says / his arm hurts.

Man   I know what he says. He just wants attention, I think.
It's –

Woman   He didn't fall or anything then?

Man   He's just tired.

Woman   Did he fall over?

Man   I would tell you –

Woman   So he didn't?

Man   I would tell you if he fell or anything. He didn't. Go to bed.

Child   But –

Man   Go to bed.

Child   You're rubbish. Simon's dad takes him to Hamleys when they go out. Says he can have anything he wants. Says he can choose anything. He's got a PS3.

Man   What's that?

Child   You don't know?

Man   Sorry. No.

Child   God.

Man   . . .

Woman   Go upstairs now.

Child   My arm hurts. Mum.

Man   You spoil him.

Woman   Would you just . . . just fucking go upstairs. Now. Please.

Child   You don't love me, Mum.

Woman   NOW.

I do not spoil him. He enjoys himself with me. What did you do? Take him to the job centre? He looks bored. He hates it with you.

Man You shouldn't swear in front of him.

Woman What have you done to his arm?

Man What have *I* done?

Woman Well, something's happened.

Man I broke it.

Woman What?

Man He was mucking about, so I took his little arm, and snapped it across my knee.

Woman What? What?

Man Like a dry twig.

Woman . . .

Man I DON'T KNOW WHAT'S WRONG WITH HIS ARM. Perhaps he trapped it in something. He's just moaning again. He's spoilt.

Woman Why did you say that?

Man You spoilt him.

Woman That you broke his arm. Like a . . . twig. Why did you say that? You're so weird. You're like a like a fucking . . .

Man Maybe it's the coke we take together.

Woman Like a fucking retard.

Man Or the violent films I show him . . .

Woman I'll tell social services. They'll stop you seeing him.

Man You won't stop me seeing my son.

Woman You said you broke his arm.

Man I was joking, you / thick bitch.

Woman   You said you take coke . . .

Man   Coca-Cola. I was taking the piss out of you.

Woman   I love him. I don't want you near him. You don't know –

Man   I would do anything for him.

Woman   You won't even take him to a toy shop.

Man   He's spoilt. You spoilt him. You changed him.

Woman   Maybe he isn't even yours.

Man   What?

Woman   Around the time he was conceived, I was having an affair. Maybe he's not yours.

Man   We never stopped fucking till I left.

Woman   Yes, I was fucking someone else. And you. Both. He was bigger.

Man   Was it Karl?

Woman   No. Someone else.

Man   Fucking slapper.

The **Woman** *hits the* **Man***.*

Woman   Your breath still smells bad. Can you leave? I don't want you looking after him again. I'm calling our solicitor. You better do the same, if you can afford it.

She faces the **Child***.*

Woman   I do love you and so does Dad.

The **Child** *thinks about this.*

Child   But Dad's a wanker, isn't he?

Woman   Yes.

I'm afraid he is.

But . . .

Child What?

Man Hi.

Other Woman I'm sorry.

Man Hi.

Other Woman Do I know you?

Man No. But . . . can I buy you . . . ?

Can I buy you . . . ?

Can I buy you a drink?

Other Woman . . .

Man . . .

Older Woman Love . . .

Other Woman If you want.

Man Thanks.

Older Woman Love –

Woman No.

Older Woman Love . . .

Woman No.

I haven't got the time.

Child What?

Woman Your dad. The person you call Dad. It might be that he isn't really. That Dad is actually someone else.

Child Really?

Woman Maybe. We'll have to do some tests. But would you like that? If he wasn't your dad any more?

Child Yeah. It would be much better. Would my new real dad take me to Hamleys on Saturdays?

Woman He might.

Child   Would he love you?

Woman   I'm with Karl.

Child   Does Karl love you?

Woman   Yes. Of course.

Child   He gets angry with you sometimes.

Woman   Sometimes we get angry with people we love, but –

Child   You get angry with me.

Woman   I'm sorry about that. I shouldn't. How's your arm?

Child   It's got a bruise on it now. Can we go to Starbucks? I want a muffin.

Older Woman   Love . . .

Woman   That means it's getting better. Starbucks? Not now, Mum.

Man   There.

Other Woman   Thanks.

Man   So, what do you do?

Other Woman   I've got a boyfriend. Thanks.

Man   I . . .

Other Woman   You were trying to chat me up, right?

Man   Yes. I suppose so.

Other Woman   I've got a boyfriend. So don't bother. Thanks for the drink.

She laughs.

Older Woman   Love . . .

Child   Mum.

Woman   What?

Child   Granny.

Woman   I know. I know. What?

The **Older Woman** *has urinated on herself.*

Woman   Oh. Mum. You're a fucking pain.

The **Woman** *starts to mop up the urine.*

Older Woman   Love . . . Sorry.

Woman   Why didn't you call someone?

Older Woman   I did.

Child   Can we go to Starbucks?

Woman   I should hire someone.

Older Woman   I hate all this.

Woman   Maybe a home then.

Older Woman   Don't be like that.

Child   Mum.

Woman   I'm coming. God, Mum, there's enough of it, isn't there?

Older Woman   You're horrible to me.

Woman   I'm joking.

Older Woman   You think this is funny?

Woman   The only way I can get through it. It's this, or not coming at all. Sorry.

Older Woman   Can't you show me the tiniest bit of love?

Woman   Not when I'm wiping you up, no. It fucking mings.

Older Woman   Don't use language like that.

Woman   Just shut up for a minute, will you?

Older Woman   Don't tell me to / shut up.

Woman   Calm down, or you'll shit yourself.

The **Older Woman** *reaches out and hits the* **Woman**. *The* **Woman** *hits her back, but not as hard.*

Young Woman   Hello.

Man   Sorry. Excuse me.

Young Woman   DVD?

Man   What?

Young Woman   Cheap DVDs. New films.

Man   New?

Child   Mum.

Young Woman   Not available in the shops. Very cheap.

Child   I want to go to Starbucks.

Man   What've you got? It's for my son.

Woman   I've got to go.

Older Woman   I'm sorry. Do come back. Sorry, love. Sorry.

Woman   I find it difficult.

Older Woman   I know. I'm a pain. You don't have to come.

Woman   Yeah, but I do, don't I?

Older Woman   I suppose you do, yes.

I appreciate it though.

Where do you have to go?

Woman   I promised I'd take him to Starbucks. He likes the muffins.

Older Woman   That's nice. Does he want to come and visit me?

Woman   He doesn't like the smell.

Older Woman   Does he talk about me?

Woman   When he was younger, he used to talk about you all the time.

Older Woman   And now?

Woman   I think he's forgotten.

Older Woman   You should bring him to visit.

Woman   I'll try . . .

Older Woman   Good.

Woman   But we're busy. Wait till Christmas, maybe.

Man   Do you want to watch a film?

Child   I'm tired.

Man   I bought you a film. It's new.

Child   I'm tired.

What?

Man   *American Pie: The Wedding.*

Child   That's not new.

Man   Have you seen it?

Child   Is it a fifteen?

Man   Um. Yeah.

Child   I'll watch it later.

Man   No. Wait. It's an eighteen.

Child   Let me see it.

Man   All right. I'll put it on now.

The video comes on.

Child   This is shit. It's just a video camera in a cinema. It's a bootleg.

Man   Wait. It'll get better.

Child   No. No. This is shit.

I want to go home now.

Man   How's your arm?

Child   Like you care. You're not my dad, anyway.

Man   What?

Child   Mum told me. You're not my dad. I won't have to come and see you any more soon.

Man   Mum's wrong. I am your dad.

Child   No you're not. You're a wanker.

Man   Don't swear like that.

Child   You can't tell me what to do.

Man   Mum's lying to you. She wants you to hate me.

Child   Can I go home now?

Man   No. It's not four o'clock. We've still got a couple of hours.

Child   I want to go home.

Man   No.

Child   Let me go, you wanker.

The **Child** *starts attacking the* **Man**. *The* **Man** *doesn't respond. The* **Child** *stops and takes a step back.*

Man   I'll get the car.

Another Woman   Excuse me.

Man   Yes.

Another Woman   Does this train go to Victoria?

Man   Um . . .

Another Woman   Is it a Circle Line train?

Man   Um . . . Yes . . . I think so.

Another Woman   Right.

Another Man   Yes, it is.

Another Woman   Thank you.

Man   I . . .

Another Woman   . . .

Man   I . . .

Another Woman   I'm sorry?

Man   Do you . . . ?

Another Woman   Are you all right?

Man   No.

Another Man   Jesus.

Another Woman   . . .

Man   I want you to tell me something.

Woman   What?

Man   Did you really have an affair?

Woman   Of course. Why do you think I wanted the test done?

Man   Because you might have slept with someone. That doesn't mean you had an affair.

Woman   This was nine years ago.

But it turns out you are his father. It doesn't matter.

Man   But this isn't about him now. I just want to know the truth.

Woman   Why?

Man   It matters to me.

Woman   Why?

Man   Whether, even though you fucked someone else, I was still the man you were emotionally faithful to.

Woman   Emotionally faithful?

Man   . . .

Woman   Emotionally faithful?

Man   Okay . . .

Woman   Are you with anyone at the moment?

Man   No.

Woman   Is this why you want to know? Because deep down you hope that underneath all this shit, and you letting me down, and me kicking you out, and my new husband, and our son who hates you, you hope that somewhere under all that I secretly still harbour a love for you that will never die.

Man   Yes. Exactly that.

Woman   And you hope that because right now you feel alone and unwanted by anyone, including your own son.

Man   Yes.

Woman   It was a fully operational affair. Sexually, emotionally and utterly unfaithful to you. I had finally realised that you were not the person I hoped you were. That you were, in fact, something less.

Man   But we still made love. You carried on with me through that.

Woman   I was desperate that we might find something to hold on to, but there wasn't. Not even a child could keep us together.

Man   No.

Woman   You know, even now, I still shudder at the thought that one day my son might remind me of you.

Man   Has he?

Woman   Not yet. Thank God.

Man   Why do you do this to me when you know I'm a good person?

Woman   That's not enough. You lack confidence. You are innocent. Stunted. You refuse to understand money, or responsibility. You are still a boy. You may be good or whatever but I want someone who knows when to buy me flowers, who pays bills for me, who isn't afraid of a spliff or outdoor sex, and I want someone who has a very clean car.

Man   I don't think you're happy.

Woman   I am. I just wish that you didn't exist.

Man   You want me dead.

Woman   I just wish that you were . . . erased.

Man   Erased.

Woman   That our son never needed you.

Man   Do you think he will?

Woman   Not if I can help it. We're starting fresh proceedings against you. That's what I wanted to say.

Man   On what grounds?

Woman   Abuse and neglect. His arm is still bruised. Either you did it, or you failed to stop it happening. Whatever, it doesn't look good for you.

Man   I can't afford a new solicitor.

Woman   I know.

Man

Woman

Man   Of course you do.

Woman   Is it worth it? Give him up. We don't need your money.

Man   He's my son.

Woman   No. He's nothing like you. He's another man's son now. You are just an unreliable irritant.

Man   Oh, fuck off.

Woman   Make sure you open your post.

Man   Yeah.

Mum?

Mother   Yes.

Man   Why did you and Dad die?

Mother   It happens.

Man   Do you miss me?

Father   Of course. We always miss you.

Mother   We watch what you do.

Man   And? What do you think?

Mum?

What should I . . .

Have you ever seen a calf being taken away from the cow, so that the cow will give milk?

Older Woman   No.

Man   It rages. The farmer tries to fend it off with a cattle prod but it endures electricity tearing its body apart to get to its child. It breaks the pen, it screams and bleeds and scrabbles around. It takes hours for it to stop.

Older Woman   All so we can drink milk.

Man   Yeah.

Older Woman   Cows are normally so . . . placid.

Man   Well, I'm like that. I won't let him go.

Older Woman   Is this why you've come to see me?

Man   She's trying to take him away.

Older Woman   Why?

Man   She says I abused him. Apparently he hurt his arm when he was out with me.

Older Woman   How?

Man   I don't know.

Older Woman   How can you not know?

Man   I didn't see . . .

Older Woman   Anyway, she doesn't listen to me. There's nothing I can do.

Man   You always said you liked me.

Older Woman   I thought you were good for her.

Man   I used to love Christmas at your house.

Older Woman   It was nice, wasn't it? It was such a shame when you two . . .

Man   Do you think she misses me?

Older Woman   I'm sure she must. Somewhere. There must be something about you she'll never find in anyone else. You're a nice man, aren't you?

Man   How can I stop her?

Older Woman   I don't know. She's not happy. But if he hurt his arm –

Man   I don't think that was with me.

Older Woman   You're nice, but you're not reliable, are you? Maybe you shouldn't really be looking after a young boy by yourself. Even for an afternoon.

Man   They swear at him.

Older Woman   I know. But –

Man   Have you met Karl?

Older Woman   Yes.

Man   What do you think?

Older Woman   He's very rich, isn't he?

Man   Is he a good man?

Older Woman   I don't know what he is.

Man   Is he a good influence on my son?

Older Woman   From what I can tell, he looks after them both extremely well. You know they're getting a new house?

Man   Yes.

Older Woman   In Notting Hill.

Man   Yes.

Older Woman   It's got a roof terrace.

Man   . . .

Older Woman   He gives them everything they need.

Man   But is he a good man?

Older Woman   He has money. That's good. He loves them both. That's good. As for being a good man . . .

Man   Morals.

Older Woman   Listen. There's no point having morals if you keep letting people down. If you can't afford to carry out the decisions you make.

Man   I try.

Older Woman   That's not enough.

Man   Will you say something to her? Will you help me?

Older Woman   I don't want to get involved. It won't make any difference anyway.

Man   Please.

Older Woman   I'm sorry.

Man   I'm desperate.

Older Woman   No.

Man   . . .

Older Woman   Can you leave now?

Man   I'll help you in return. I'll come and visit and help you to stay. You won't have to go into a home.

Older Woman   She wouldn't like you coming here.

Man   What can I do?

Older Woman   Nothing, nothing. You shouldn't have come to me. It's not right. This isn't my business. Leave me alone.

Man   It is to do with you. It's your grandson. Don't you care?

Older Woman   Look. I want you to leave now.

Man   I won't give up.

Older Woman   Can you leave my house? Please. Now.

Man   Don't you understand?

Older Woman   Get out.

Man   Look –

Older Woman   You're frightening me.

Man   I'm not frightening you. I'm trying to make you understand. You would never have given up your daughter. I'm just doing what is natural.

Older Woman   Stand further away. I can believe you abused him.

Man   What?

Older Woman   I can believe it. Waving your arms around.

Man   No.

Older Woman   Maybe you are a violent man.

Man   No.

Older Woman   She was right to leave you. I don't know you at all. Get out.

She hits the **Man***. She goes to do it again. He grabs her arm.*

Older Woman   I'll scream.

Man   Do you *want* to move out of here? To be sat in a home? In your own shit, until someone comes to change you? One of those people you see just sat there waiting to die?

I can look after you. Keep you here at home. Keep you happy. I promise. If you help me first. I'll look after you. I promise.

I'm your only option.

Do you understand?

Older Woman   Hello.

Child   Hello.

Older Woman   I'm really glad you came to visit me.

Child   Yeah.

Older Woman   It can get a bit lonely here all by myself.

Child   Yeah.

Older Woman   What are you up to?

Child   What do you mean?

Older Woman   Well . . . at school.

Child   Um . . . not much. Gavin's got a projector. We play games.

Older Woman   What's a projector?

Child   I want one.

Older Woman   What is it?

Child   Will you buy me one?

Older Woman   I don't know what it is.

Child   It projects stuff. Onto the wall.

Older Woman   I see.

Child   Will you buy me one?

Older Woman   You'll have to ask your mother.

Child   What's that smell?

Older Woman   I don't know.

Child   I only smell it here. Smells like a toilet.

Older Woman   It's rude to mention it.

Child   What is it? Have you wet yourself?

Older Woman   . . .

Child   . . .

Older Woman   Yes.

Child   . . .

Older Woman   If you ask these things you must expect an honest answer.

Child   That's gross.

Older Woman   That's what it's like being old.

Child   What's wrong with you?

Older Woman   My bladder won't hold in the urine.

Child   Sick.

Older Woman   Yes. I'm ill. Getting worse, too.

Child   Are you going to die?

Older Woman   Yes.

Child   When?

Older Woman   Soon.

Child   Now?

Older Woman   Maybe. Soon.

Child   I don't understand.

Older Woman   Love.

Woman   Hang on.

Child   Mum.

Woman   What?

Child   I don't get it.

Older Woman   Love.

Woman   No. Mum. No. Mum.

Older Woman   Love.

Woman   What did you tell him?

Older Woman   The truth. Where is he?

Woman   He's at a friend's house now. He didn't want to come again. You scared him last time.

Older Woman   How are you getting on?

Woman   Fine.

Older Woman   Do you see his father much?

Woman   Every Saturday.

Older Woman   It's important a boy sees his father, isn't it?

Woman   Not when his father is a dangerous twat, no.

Older Woman   You shouldn't talk like that.

Woman   Please get over it, Mum. Watch some television. This is the twenty-first century. This is how we speak.

Older Woman   He may have his flaws but, well, he is the boy's . . .

Woman   Two weeks ago, when my son came back, he had a bruise on his arm.

Older Woman   Well, you don't know –

Woman   It's still there. It isn't going away.

Older Woman   You don't know –

Woman   I know enough. I've seen it. Why do you think I kicked him out?

Older Woman   I just think you shouldn't try to stop him seeing his own son.

Woman   How did you know I wanted to?

Older Woman   I . . .

Woman   How did you know that?

Older Woman   . . .

Woman   Listen to me. How did you know?

Older Woman   I –

Woman   Stay out of my life.

Older Woman   I guessed that you would.

Woman   No.

Older Woman   . . .

Woman   From him?

Older Woman

Woman   Has he spoken to you? Visited you here?

Older Woman   He –

Woman   Fucking –

Older Woman   He was worried.

Woman   What did he tell you?

Older Woman   He just wants to keep in contact. He wanted me to have a word.

Woman   Why would you do that?

Older Woman   I –

Woman   Did you tell him I don't give a shit what you think? Why would you even try?

Older Woman   I just thought –

Woman   I fucking hate you / for what you used to do to me.

Older Woman   Don't swear.

Woman   Don't you dare tell me how to be a parent. You were useless. What you did to me.

Older Woman   I looked after you.

Woman   You scared me. I used to hope Dad would get drunk because it might mean he stood up for himself. You made him small. When he died –

Older Woman   I don't –

Woman   When he died, I bet his last breath was a sigh of relief that you had finally shut the fuck up.

Older Woman

Woman

Young Woman   Hello.

Man   Hello.

Young Woman   Looking for company?

Man   Yes.

Some company.

Young Woman   If you pay me. I don't care.

Man   Oh. Right. No. Sorry.

Older Woman   I still don't think that you should ruin your son's life for your own personal reasons.

Woman   I don't want you near him any more.

Older Woman   Don't say that.

Woman   You could only do bad things to us.

Older Woman   No. Please.

No.

I had to do it.

I had to try. He threatened me.

Woman   He . . .

Older Woman   He threatened me. Held my arm tightly. Said if I didn't help him, he would put me in a home.

Woman   He can't do that.

Older Woman   I was confused.

He made me.

Woman   Write this down. I need this.

Older Woman   Yes.

Man   She's fucking lying. I didn't do anything like that.

Woman   You went round to her house.

Man   Yes.

Woman   You wanted her to talk me into stopping proceedings.

Man   Yes.

Woman   Did you touch her?

Man   . . .

Woman   Did you touch her?

Man   Jesus.

Woman   Did you hold her arm?!

Man   She hit me and I restrained her.

Woman   She's in a fucking wheelchair.

Man   She got upset.

Woman   Why?

Man   She thought . . . I don't know.

Woman   Did you threaten her?

Man   I offered to help her.

Woman   She's scared of you.

Man   I didn't want to upset her.

Woman   This will count against you. She will tell them what you did.

Man   Please. You know me. You know I wouldn't hurt anyone. I just want to see my son.

Woman

Man   I don't know what to do.

Woman   Start again. Somewhere else. Without us.

Man   No.

Young Woman   What shall I do?

Man   Just sit with me.

Young Woman   Okay.

Man   . . .

. . .

. . .

Just having you here makes me feel dirty. Sorry.

Young Woman   Doesn't bother me.

Man   Are you happy? Doing . . . what you do?

Young Woman   Selling DVDs?

Man   No. I mean. This.

Young Woman   Of course not.

Man   Do you have a boyfriend?

Young Woman   Yes.

Man   Does he hit you?

Young Woman   No.

Man   Do you take drugs together?

Young Woman   Sometimes.

Man   Does he love you?

Young Woman   Very much.

Man   Why do you do this then?

Young Woman   Our son is a baby. We have to live.

Man   What's your son's name?

Young Woman   Nikolai.

Man   Nikolai. You must love him very much.
To do this.

Young Woman   Of course. I would die for him.

Man   Of course you would.

Young Woman   . . .

Man   Of course . . .

Young Woman   . . .

Man   Actually . . .

Young Woman   . . .

Man   . . .

Young Woman   Yes?

Man   . . .

Young Woman   . . .

Man   . . . can I have a blow job, please?

Young Woman   Of course.

She goes to give him a blow job.

After a few moments, she looks up at him.
Something's wrong.

Woman   Where is he?

Child   Where are we going?

Where are we going?

Woman   Where is he?

Child   Where are we going?

Man   Be quiet.

Child   Where are we going?

Woman   Where's he gone?

Older Woman   What?

Man   I said shut up.

Woman   It's gone four o'clock.

Child   Where are we going?

Man   We're not going back home today.

Child   What?

Woman   Where is he?

Man   We're not going back.

Child Does Mum know?

Man No.

Child I want to go home.

Man You can't.

Child I want to. You let me.

Man You can't.

Child Let me go, you wanker.

Man Don't swear.

Child Let me go. Now.

The **Man** *goes to the* **Child** *and ties his hands behind his back.*

Child Ow.

It hurts.

Woman Hello?

Man He's fine. He's with me.

Woman What the fuck are you doing?

Man He's staying with me.

Woman Bring him back.

Man I can't. He'll be safe.

Woman You bring him back, or I'll fucking castrate you. /
I'll take an axe to your skull.

Man You made me do this.

Child Mum.

Woman Is that him?

Man Yes.

Woman Where are you?

Man You know why I had to do this, don't you?

Woman   You're not clever enough. We'll find you.

Man   Do you want to say goodbye to him?

Woman   . . .

. . .

Yes.

Child   Hello.

Woman   I'm coming to get you.

Child   Dad's tied my hands up.

Woman   Your dad's being a wanker, but I'm coming to get you soon. Don't worry.

Child   All right. I love you, Mummy.

Woman   I love you too.

Child   Goodbye.

Woman   Don't say that.

Don't . . .

Hello?

Hello?

Child   Where are we?

Man   I can't tell you that.

Child   Are we in Britain?

Man   I can't tell you. I'm sorry.

Child   I'm bored. I haven't been outside for ages.

Man   It'll be a while yet.

Child   You go out.

Man   I go to get food.

Child   I think Mum will find me.

Man   What makes you think that?

Child   She's clever.

Man   So am I.

Child   You're stupid.

Man   No. How do you know that?

Child   What?

Man   What makes you think I'm stupid?

Child   You are.

Man   No. You've been told that I'm stupid. Mum told you that. Didn't she?

Child   Yeah.

Man   You see.

Child   Because you are.

Man   No.

Child   You're thick. I've seen you in shops. On the Tube. You don't know stuff. People look at you like you're special or something.

Man   Don't say things like that. It's horrible.

Child   So Mum'll find you because she's cleverer than you.

Man   We'll see.

Child   I miss her.

Man   I'm sorry.

Child   I've never missed you.

Man   You've never really known me.

Child   I've been out with you every week of my life. I think I do.

Man   There's loads of stuff you don't know about me.

Child   Like what?

Man   I got a first in philosophy from Bristol University.

I lived in America for two years.

I can make kites.

I used to be the best in my street at arcade games.

You probably don't even know what they are, do you?

Child

Man   I was in the rugby A-team at school.

I used to own a motorbike –

Child   I knew some of that already.

Man   But not all of it.

Child   No. But I don't really care.

Man   Don't you want to get to know me?

Child   No.

I don't think I like you.

Man   What do you like?

Child   I don't know.

Man   Come on.

Child   Having fun.

Man   When do you have fun?

Child   With my friends at school.

Man   What do you do with them?

Child   Stuff.

Man   What else?

Child   When we went to the wrestling.

Man   Did Karl take you?

Child   Yeah.

Man   What did you like about that?

Child   It's cool.

Man   Okay.

Child   We was shouting at them, and one comes over to us, and says he's going to rip Dad's head off cos he said he was pussy.

Man   Dad.

Child   . . .

Man

Child   Yeah.

Man   You call him 'Dad'.

Child   Yeah. He wanted me to.

Man   . . .

Child   Well, he is really, isn't he?

Man   No. He's not.

Child   Yeah, he is. Really. I mean, like you are, but . . . most of the time you're not there so −

Man   It's different now.

Child   No. Mum'll find us. Or Dad will. He'll find you and if he doesn't kill you, you'll get sent to prison.

Man   Would you care?

Child   If he killed you?

No.

Man   I think you would a bit.

Child   No.

Man   Do you remember when we went out and had fun?

Child   No. I've forgotten.

Man   Do you remember going down the station and watching the trains? Counting the carriages. You used to love that.

Child   No. I hated it. It was shit.

Man   That's not true.

Child   Trains? God.

Man   And we used to have races in the park. Who could get from tree to tree first.

Child   I know.

Man   You liked it.

Child   It was all right.

Man   Yeah. Remember?

Child   It was all right. It wasn't that good. I was a kid.

Man   Maybe we can have fun again, now?

Child   No.

Man   Somewhere in you, you still love me.

Child   Shut up. No.

Woman   I miss you.

Child   I miss you too, Mum.

Man   It'll pass. It'll get better.

Woman   I don't think we'll find them.

Older Woman   I'm sorry for what I did.

Woman   I'm so scared.

Older Woman   You can talk to me.

Woman   I don't want to.

Older Woman   He'll look after him.

Woman   He'll try. But I'm scared what will happen when he fails.

Older Woman   He loves him.

Woman   That's not enough. You used to tell me you loved me.

Older Woman   I do.

Woman   See?

Most people really have no idea.

Man   I remember the night you were born. Your mother was all sweaty and tired. She was beautiful. We sat on the bed, with you in our arms. We named you, and I planned our future together. Maybe a brother or sister to come. A bigger house. Holidays. Grandchildren. She fell asleep, so did you, and I watched you both all night. I thought I had become someone different that night. I was a father, a grown-up. A man. I would protect you both for ever. I would always make sure you were safe. Both of you. Of course it turns out now she had already been sleeping with someone else. It turns out that maybe she was just a slut all along.

Woman   I'm dreaming of you.

Man   Are you?

Woman   Not you.

Child   Mum.

Woman   You.

Child   I'm dreaming of playing on the Xbox with you.

Woman   Me too.

Child   Are you?

Woman   Who's winning?

Child   Me.

Woman   Of course.

Child   You're a bit rubbish.

Man   I wish I did that with you.

Woman   . . .

Child   . . .

Man   Don't you two remember the good times?

Woman   There were a few.

Child   When we went to that theme park.

Man   Don't they count for anything?

Woman   No.

Child   I don't want to be here.

Man   Well, I'm starting something new.

Woman   I suppose you are.

Child   Mum.

Man   Are you awake?

Child   I want Mum. I want to go home.

Man   I'll look after you.

Child   No. It's not the same. What about my friends?

Man   You'll make new ones.

Child   No.

My arm.

Man   Is it still . . . ?

Child   It's gone black.

Man   Let me have a look.

Child   It's getting worse. It really hurts.

Man   Did you go to a doctor?

Child   He said it was a sprain.

Man   Sprains don't go black.

Child   What's wrong with me?

Man   I don't know.

Child   I should go to hospital.

Man   We can't. You can't leave the house.

Child   Don't you care?

Man   Of course . . . but . . .

Child   I might die.

Man   If I let you go now, I'll never see you again. Ever.

Child   What if I die?

Man   That won't happen.

Child   How do you know?

Man   We'll give it a couple of days.

Child   Then what?

Man   We'll give it a couple of days.

Child   Karl will be after you by now.

Man   I'm scared.

Child   He'll find you.

Man   Will he?

Child   Yes. Why don't you stop now? Give yourself up.

Man   No.

Child   You wouldn't go to prison.

Man   Yes I would, and they would never let me see you again.

Child   Why do you want to see me? / I'm horrible to you.

Man   You're my son.

Why are you so horrible to me?

Child   You left us.

Man   Your mum kicked me out. I wanted to stay.

Child   You're not very good. I want a dad that's strong. And rich.

Man   Are those things really important to you?

Child   Yeah.

You don't even like football.

Man   No.

Child   So who would take me?

Man   Who do you support?

Child   You don't even know.

Man   I wanted you to read books. / To like art.

Child   I don't like books. They're gay.

I'm good at art.

Man   Are you?

Child   Yeah. I showed you my picture. Don't you remember?

Man   Yes. Now I do. It was great.

Child   I got an A.

Man   I bet.

Child   Yeah.

Woman   It won't be long before someone sees him. His photo was on the news.

Older Woman   It's sad.

Woman   Karl's out now. He says he'll find him before the police.

Older Woman   What will he do if he finds him?

Woman   I don't care. I want my son back.

Older Woman   Are you all right, love?

Woman   No.

Older Woman   Come here.

Woman   No.

Older Woman   I'll hug you.

Woman   It's too late for you to start that now.

Older Woman   Maybe I've changed.

Woman   . . .

Older Woman   It's not too late.

Give me a chance.

Give me a fucking chance.

Woman   God.

Mum.

God.

Older Woman   You see, love.

I have changed.

I've been watching fucking television.

Child   We're in Scotland.

Man   What makes you think that?

Child   I heard someone go past, first thing this morning.
They had a Scottish accent.

Man   Maybe.

Child   What's that?

Man   A bandage for your arm.

Child   It's worse.

Man   We'll give it another day.

Child   I'll shout all night for help.

Man   No one will hear you. Put this on.

Child   I just want it to stop.

Man   Swallow this. It'll help the pain.

Woman   What about his arm?

Another Woman   I know him. I know that man. He
looked . . .

Another Man   Jesus.

Another Woman   Lonely.

Man   Does that feel better?

Child   Yes. Thank you. Thanks, Dad.

The **Man** *kisses the* **Child** *on the forehead.*

Man   I'm so sorry about all this. I really am.

Child   I know.

Man   Is there a bit of you that loves me? Somewhere?

Child   . . .

Man   Or at least feels sorry for me.

Child   I do. I do feel sorry for you.
Maybe I love you. I don't know.

I wouldn't want to never see you again.

I do remember the trains.

I didn't enjoy it. Even then. I found it boring.

But I do remember it.

And I remember how much you liked it.

And at the time that made me happy.

The door of the room opens and **Karl** *walks in, from outside.*

Karl   So it is you.

Surprise.

Man   Stay in the other room.

Child   No.

Karl   What did your mum tell you when you were young?

Be kind?

Polite?

Well?

Well?

What did she tell you?

Man   She told me to be good.

Karl   Yeah.

Sit down.

Good.

Because we need to have a talk about –

Man   I'm not letting him go.

Karl   Um.

Sit down.

Good.

Because we need to talk, don't we?

When I was young and I did something wrong, my dad used to hit me round the back of the head. That was a good lesson. It taught me about consequences. We know all about consequences, don't we?

Child   Yeah.

Karl   That you have to take responsibility for what you do.

Do you agree?

Man   How did you find me?

Karl   Do you agree?

Man   Yes.

Karl   Good. I went to your flat the night you left. Just pushed open your door cos the lock's not working. You should fix that. I checked your computer. And I found that it still had on it all the holiday homes in Scotland you'd been trying to book. So that narrowed it down.

Man   What about the police?

Karl   I took your computer with me.

I wanted to find you first. But they won't be long now.

Man   Is she with you?

Karl   No.

Man   Does she know you're here?

Karl   Not yet.

Man   What do you want, then?

You're not taking him away.

Karl   Yes.

But that's not what we're going to talk about now.

Man   No. He's staying with me.

Karl   We're going to talk about how you make it up to my wife. And me and my son.

Child   Dad . . .

Karl   My son.

Man   He's not.

Child   Dad.

Man   Stop it.

Karl   His arm's black.

Man   . . .

Karl   You left his arm to rot.

Man   No.

Karl   You left his arm to rot.

You are a lame cunt.

Aren't you?

Man   Shut up.

Karl   So what are you going to do? To make amends.

Man   . . .

Karl   You're going tell him that you hope his arm gets better. Then you're going to say goodbye to my son.

Man   No.

Karl   You will. Or I'll tear your arm off with my hands.

Man   No.

Karl   Say goodbye.

Man   No. Come here.

Karl   Stay there. Say goodbye.

Man   Fuck you.

Karl   Don't swear in front of him.

Man   Get out.

Now.

Karl *grabs his arm, and twists it.*

Karl   Say goodbye.

Say goodbye.

Say goodbye.

Child   Dad . . .

Karl   Say goodbye.

Say goodbye.

Say goodbye.

Child   Dad.

Karl   Go to the car.

Child   No. Dad. Stop it.

Karl   Get into the car now.

Child   Stop. Fucking stop.

He breaks up the two men.

It's not right.

Karl   Your mum's been crying. She's probably crying right now.

Child   Yeah. But I don't like it.

Karl   Go outside. Get in the car. I'll be there in a minute.

Child   . . .

Karl   It's all right. We're just going to talk.

I thought you liked wrestling.

Child   . . .

Karl   Little pussy, aren't you?

Child   No.

Karl   Go and get in the car, then.

Child   Okay.

Karl   You not going to say goodbye?

Child   Goodbye, Dad.

Man   I'll see you in a minute.

Child   He's going to kill you now, I think.

Man   I'll see you in a minute.

Child   Goodbye, Dad.

Man

Karl   Little pussy.

Man   Don't call him that.

Karl   I'm doing him a favour. If he learns how life works now, he will be happy. He will be a success.

Man

Karl

Man   So what now?

Karl   When the police get here I'll say you refused to let him go.

I did what I had to.

Stand up.

The **Man** *stands.*

Karl   Come here.

If you don't I'll make it worse.

Karl *hits the* **Man**.

*The **Man** falls to the ground.*

Karl   Stand up.

Come here.

*The **Man** stands. Walks towards **Karl**.*

Karl *hits him hard.*

*The **Man** falls to the ground.*

Karl   Stand up.

Come here.

*The **Man** stands. Walks towards **Karl**.*

Karl *hits him hard.* **Karl** *laughs.*

Karl   Stand up.

Come here.

*The **Man** stands, just.*

Child   Dad. Stop it.

*The **Man** rages. He tears up the room. He tries to beat up **Karl**. He throws every object at him. **Karl** just stands, watching. Occasionally pushing him away.*

*The **Man** beats and beats at **Karl**. Destroys everything in the room. Eventually there is nothing left that he can do and he runs out of energy and sits on the floor.*

Child   Are you all right?

. . .

Dad?

Man   Yes.

Child   I told you he was tough.

Man   He likes wrestling.

Child   Yeah. I'm sorry he hit you.

Man   . . .

Child   Why did it take so long to fight back?

Man   I don't agree with it.

Child   You have to fight back, or you get beaten up.

Man   Sometimes it's best not to.

Child   And get messed up?

Man   Yeah.

Child   Doesn't work. Your nose looks broken.

Man   Maybe . . .

Child   Look.

Man   Yeah. Where is he?

Child   He's gone out. To make a phone call.

Man   I'm surprised he left you here with me.

Child   He's not scared of you.

Man   No.

Child   Are you going to do anything else? To keep me here?
Now.

Man   Like what?

Child   I don't know. Get a knife.

Kill him.

Man   Would you like that?

Child   No.

Man   Then why ask?

Child   I liked it when you were fighting him.

Man   Why?

Child   It was good.

Man   Were you proud of me?

Child   Yeah.

It was like you were a wrestler. Going mental.

Man   I'm not proud of it.

Child   Okay.

Karl   It's your mum. Want to talk to her?

Child   Mum?

Woman   Steven.

Oh my God.

The **Child** *starts crying.*

Woman   Oh my God.

Are you all right?

Are you all right?

Are you all right?

Child   My arm still hurts.

Woman   Karl's going to take you to a hospital now.

Listen to me. It's all right.

Oh God. Oh God. Oh God. Oh God.

What did he do to you?

Child   They had a fight.

Woman   I know.

Child   Dad, Karl, won easily.

Woman   Yes.

Child   But real Dad. He went mental too. It was good.

Karl   Come on.

Woman   Come here.

*The **Child** runs from the **Man** to the **Woman**. **Karl** joins them.*

Woman   You're safe.

Man   . . .

Child   Mum.

Woman   My child.

Child   Dad.

Woman   I know.

Man   Goodbye.

Bye.

Mum?

Mother   Yes.

Man   Why did you tell me all this?

Mother   All what?

Man   That it is better to be polite. To put others first. Not to be violent. To turn the other cheek. Not to treat people as rivals but as friends. To try to be moral and good, and not selfish.

To love.

Mother   Because it's right.

Man   No. It's not.

Look at me.

It's not how the world is.

Father   No. It's not.

But your mother and I are still agreed.

That it's right.

Man But it doesn't work.

Does it?

Blackout.